Craft Workshop

Models

Helen Bliss & Ruth Thomson

 Crabtree Publishing Company

Craft Workshop

Crabtree Publishing Company

350 Fifth Avenue	360 York Road, R.R.4	73 Lime Walk
Suite 3308	Niagara-on-the-Lake	Headington, Oxford
New York, NY 10118	Ontario L0S 1J0	England OX3 7AD

Edited by **Virginia Mainprize**
Designed and illustrated by **Mei Lim**
Photography by **Steve Shott**

Childrens models made by
Daniel Bergsagel, Ilana Bergsagel, Angelica Bergese, Louise Bergese, Camilla Bliss-Williams, Raffy Bliss-Williams, Florrie Campbell, Laetitia Cook, Saskia Kurer, Sunny Mahotra, Freddie Mohun-Himmelweit, Bonnie Robinson, Miranda Segal, Amy Williams, Sarah Wills

Created by
Thumbprint Books

Copyright © 1998 Thumbprint Books

Cataloging-in-Publication Data

Bliss, Helen, 1955-
Models / Helen Bliss & Ruth Thomson
p. cm. – (Craft Workshop)
Includes index.
Summary: Presents a variety of models from around the world, explains why they were created,and provides instructions for making models, including such projects as a toy theater, a model room and stick creatures.
ISBN 0-86505-788-5 (pbk). – ISBN 0-86505-778-8 (rhb)
1. Models and modelmaking– Juvenile literature. [1. Models and modelmaking. 2.Handicraft.]
I. Thomson, Ruth, 1949- . II. Title. III. Series.
TT154.B56 1998 745.5928--dc21 97-32135
CIP
AC

First published in 1998 by
A & C Black (Publishers) Limited
35 Bedford Row, London WC1R 4JH

Printed in Hong Kong by Wing King Tong Co Ltd

Cover photograph: This imaginative mermaid was made by Josefina Aguilar, a Mexican craftsperson who specializes in making painted clay figures.

Contents

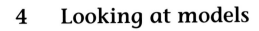

4   Looking at models

6   Tools and tricks

8   Busy bodies

10   Fancy figures

12   Sticks and bricks

14   Different dwellings

16   All sorts of animals

18   Wild and wonderful

20   Wheels and waves

22   Recycled racers

24   Imaginary creatures

26   Fierce and fantastic

28   Models in action

30   Moving models

32   Index

Looking at models

Have you ever played with toy animals, cars, space figures or a dolls' house? These are models—small copies of real or imaginary things. People make models for many reasons.

All over the world, adults make models of boats, weapons, and tools for their children. Children have fun and learn useful skills playing with these toys.

Models are also made to show what full-sized objects will look like. In the past, furniture was made by hand and was very expensive. Because there were no photographs, furniture makers made tiny models of chairs and tables. Customers looked at the models and chose the pieces they wanted to buy.

Architects make models to show how a building will look.

Some people decorate their houses with models. Others have models of real animals or imaginary creatures to give them luck or protect them from evil spirits.

Some models are made just for fun. Building model airplanes and trains are favorite hobbies.

Sailors used to keep busy on long sea voyages making small ships in bottles to bring home to their families and friends.

Models tell you a lot about the history, way of life and beliefs of the people who built them.

You will learn how to make models using clay, salt dough, wood, fabric and cardboard. Start saving cloth scraps, sticks, boxes, plastic containers and anything that looks interesting to recycle into your own original designs.

Many models are made to look exactly like the larger thing they represent. Others are not so detailed. Some are pretty, others are funny or scary. Models can be made from gold or silver or from everyday things such as paper, leather, wood or clay.

The pictures in this book of models made by children will help you get started. You can look in other books, museums and stores to find more ideas for making models.

In some parts of the world, people collect garbage for making models. They recycle wire, cloth scraps, bottles and waste paper into useful objects. In this book, you can find out about models from all over the world. You can discover why they were built.

Tools and tricks

For the projects in this book, you will need modeling clay, cardboard, balsa wood, paint, scissors, glue, masking tape and a needle and thread.

Start collecting boxes, plastic bottles and scraps of colored cloth. The instructions for making each model will tell you what you need.

Working with clay

You can use either oven-bake modeling clay, which is already colored, or self-hardening clay, which can be painted. Before you use clay, roll it in your hands until it is soft.

How to join two pieces of clay

Using a knife, scratch the two pieces you want to join, like this.

Wet both pieces and press them together. Smooth the clay with your fingers so the join doesn't show. This keeps the pieces together when they dry.

How to make salt dough

You need:
3 cups (750 ml) of flour
1 cup (250 ml) of salt
1 cup (250 ml) of water
Poster paint or food coloring
Mixing bowl, cup and wooden spoon

Mix the flour and salt together in the mixing bowl. Mix the water and some paint or food coloring in a cup.

Make a dent in the flour and salt and pour in the colored water. Mix well with the spoon and then with your hands, until the mixture is no longer sticky. If it feels too wet, add more flour. If it feels too dry, add water, a few drops at a time. If you want salt dough in different colors, make a separate batch for each one.

Join the pieces of salt dough together in the same way as modeling clay. When you have made your models, ask an adult to help you put them in the oven at 250°F (120°C) for two to three hours.

How to make papier mâché

Tear newspaper into 1 inch (3 cm) pieces. Put some flour into a mixing bowl. Stir in enough water to make a paste about as thick as yogurt. Brush on a thick layer of paste all over your model. Cover it with a layer of newspaper. Brush on more paste and stick on another layer of newspaper. Keep doing this until you have five layers.

How to join cardboard

Cut masking tape the length of the pieces of cardboard you want to join.

Press the edge along one piece of cardboard, as shown.

Hold the second piece of cardboard at a right angle to the first. Press the tape along it.

Turn the cardboard over and put another piece of tape along the outside edges.

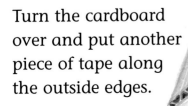

Running stitch

Thread a needle and knot the end of the thread. Pin two pieces of cloth with their right sides together. Push the needle through both layers of cloth, about ½ inch (1 cm) from the edge and pull it out again.

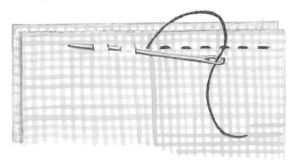

A little distance away, push the needle back to the other side to make a stitch. Keep doing this to make a line of stitches. When you are finished, sew several stitches on top of each other to keep your sewing from coming undone. Turn the piece inside out.

Hemming

Fold over about ½ inch (1 cm) of fabric. Sew a running stitch close to the edge.

Painting with primer

Use white acrylic paint or poster paint to cover the printing on boxes. Let it dry before using colored paints. The colors will be much stronger.

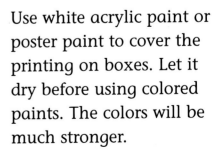

Busy bodies

Models of people are created for many reasons. Some are made as dolls or pieces for games. Others are made to help teach people about their past and religion.

The chess pieces shown above are models of people in two Indian armies. They are set out as if they were on a battlefield. The kings and their chief officers sit under canopies on top of elephants.

Each army has soldiers riding horses, camels or elephants. These chess pieces are made of ivory, painted bright colors and decorated with gold. How are they different from a modern chess set?

This decorated wooden box comes from Peru. It is called a *retablo*. It shows country people having fun at a celebration known as a fiesta. The models are made of plaster mixed with mashed potato. They are brushed with glue before being painted bright colors.

Retablos first told stories from the Bible and about the lives of Christian saints. The Spanish, who conquered Peru in the 1500s, used retablos to teach people about the Christian religion.

Two hundred years ago, peddlers traveled from village to village selling things people could not make for themselves. This German peddler doll is selling buttons, thread, cheese graters and pot holders.

The fathers and uncles of North American Hopi children carve these *kachina* dolls. The dolls teach the children about kachina spirits that the Hopis believe bring rain, good crops, health, happiness and a long life.

There are over two hundred kachina spirits. Each one looks different and has special powers. The dolls hang in homes. Hopi children are taught to recognize each kachina.

Fancy figures

Create a stuffed peddler doll selling odds and ends, or make a painted kachina doll to hang in your room. You can build a story box to show a special event you would like to remember.

Peddler doll

You may need an adult to help you with this project.

1 The body

Half-fill a plastic pop bottle with sand or dried beans and screw on the top. Cut the legs off an old pair of pantyhose. Fill the toe of one leg with cotton wool. Pull the leg over the top of the bottle.

2 The head

Make the doll's head by winding thread around the stuffed toe. Glue on a felt nose, mouth, eyes and wooly hair. Sew the tights together under the base of the bottle.

3 The arms

Cut a rectangle from the other leg of the pantyhose. Sew together the long edges and one end. Turn the tube inside out. Stuff it and sew up the other end. Sew the tube to the doll's back.

4 The dress

Fold a piece of cloth in half. Lay the doll on top. With a felt-tipped pen, draw a wide dress shape with a neck hole at the top. Cut out the dress. Stitch the sides and arms together. Sew up the hem. (See page 7 for instructions for sewing a running stitch and hem.) Pull the dress over the doll and tie a ribbon around her waist. Make a bonnet, a cape and an apron.

5 The tray

Tape ribbon to both sides of the lid of a small box. Fill the tray with odds and ends.

Story box

With masking tape, attach cardboard doors to the sides of a box. (See page 7 for instructions for joining cardboard.) For the roof, attach a triangle of cardboard, as long as the top, to the box. Paint the box white.

When the paint is dry, paint on bold flowers and patterns. Shape people, animals and other objects from self-hardening clay. Let them dry before you paint them. Glue them inside the story box.

Kachina doll

Shape a body from a large ball of salt dough. (See page 6.) Shape a head, arms and legs from smaller pieces of dough. Attach them to the body. (See page 6 for instructions for joining two pieces of clay.)

Place the doll on a greased cookie sheet. Ask an adult to put it in the oven. (See page 6 for salt dough instructions.)

When the doll has cooled, paint it. Glue on cloth scraps and add a headdress of feathers and sticks.

Sticks and bricks

For thousands of years, people have built tiny copies of houses and buildings. Some were used as decoration, others were put into the tombs of the dead. Today, they are made mostly as toys.

Room arranged by Lois Heath, with objects from the Kristin Baybars collection

Making dolls' houses is a popular hobby. The room in the picture above looks like a country kitchen fifty years ago. In fact, the dolls' house and everything in it are new.

Dolls' houses and tiny rooms have been made as toys for over three hundred years. In the past, they were often copies of grand houses, filled with tiny models of fine furniture.

A spirit house, such as this one, stands outside most buildings in Thailand. Some look like small temples. Other are models of houses. Thai people believe that the spirits which guard a place live in the spirit house. Every day, people bring the spirits food and flowers.

Native North Americans from the plains lived in large tepees made of long poles covered with buffalo skins. Young girls played with tiny toy tepees.

These tepees were decorated with pictures with special meanings. Inside, there were small animal-skin carpets and tiny cooking pots. Playing with these objects taught girls some of the skills they would need when they grew up.

In ancient China, important people were buried in large and beautiful tombs. Many of their possessions were buried with them.

Thieves often broke into the tombs to steal anything valuable. After a while, because of this, people were buried instead with small models of things that had been important during their lifetime.

Different dwellings

You, too, can make tiny buildings. You can build a model room, or a spirit house or set up a tepee camp. These are great projects to make with a friend.

Tiny treasures

Cut off the top and one side of a large cardboard box. Paint the inside and outside white. When it is dry, paint wallpaper patterns on the walls and paint the floor.

Shape cakes, fruit, plates and cups from oven-bake modeling clay. (See page 7 for instructions for joining two pieces of clay.)

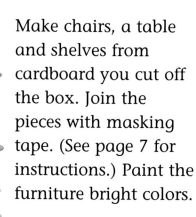

Make chairs, a table and shelves from cardboard you cut off the box. Join the pieces with masking tape. (See page 7 for instructions.) Paint the furniture bright colors.

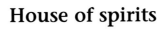

House of spirits

Draw two doors on the side of a cardboard box. Ask an adult to help you cut them open. Cut a steep roof and decorations from cardboard. Attach them to the box with masking tape. (See page 7 for instructions for joining cardboard.) Paint the house bright colors.

A tepee camp

For each tepee, collect six twigs about 12 inches (30 cm) long. (If you can't find sticks, use barbecue sticks or straws.) Arrange the sticks in the shape of a tepee. Wind a piece of string tightly around the sticks, about 2 inches (5 cm) below the top, as shown.

Cut a semi-circle of cloth about 10 inches (25 cm) in diameter. Cut a small semi-circle in the center of the straight edge, big enough for the sticks to poke through.

10 in
25 cm

Paint the cloth in earthy colors with pictures of the sun, the moon and birds. Fit the cloth over the sticks.

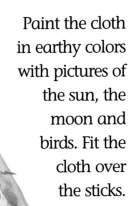

15

All sorts of animals

All over the world, people make models of animals. They can be made from almost anything and come in all shapes and sizes. You may have toy animals of your own.

Colorful wooden animals, such as these ants and this lizard, come from farming villages in southern Mexico. The whole family works together to make these carved models.

The father and older boys carve the animals from soft wood. The young children and grandparents sand them smooth. The mother and older girls paint the animals bright colors.

These painted wooden birds are called decoys. Hunters use them to attract ducks and other water birds. The duck decoy is hollow so it can float on lakes and ponds. The egret decoy is made of wood and metal tied together with string. It stands in the middle of grassy marshes on a sharp stick.

Decoys were first used by North American native people. They made them from reeds and feathers.

In Japan, many restaurants and stores have a white cat near the door. The cat is made of china or papier mâché. Japanese people think it brings good luck. The cat holds up one paw as if it were trying to catch money from customers.

Potters in Russia make these painted animals as toys, whistles and decorations. More than a thousand years ago, small clay animals like these were made as statues of the gods. A horse with three heads and decorated with circles was a statue of the sun god. The spots on these modern horses copy the decorations on the horse sun god.

Wild and wonderful

Try making your own model
animals. Collect strangely
shaped pieces of wood to turn into
weird creatures. You can also shape
funny clay animals or make a lucky
cat box to keep your money safe.

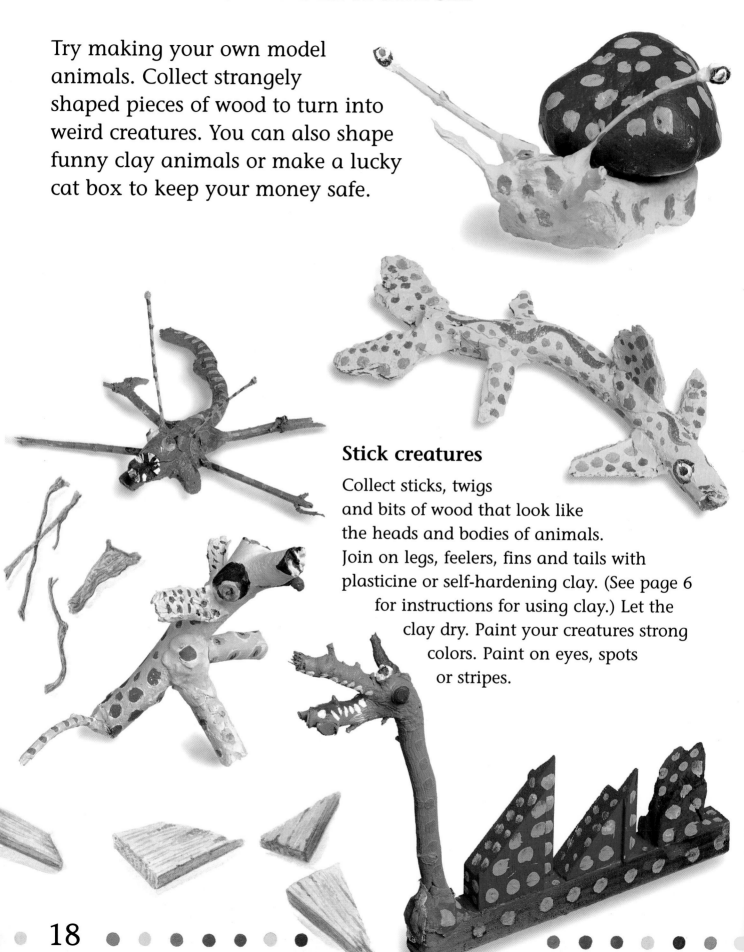

Stick creatures

Collect sticks, twigs
and bits of wood that look like
the heads and bodies of animals.
Join on legs, feelers, fins and tails with
plasticine or self-hardening clay. (See page 6
for instructions for using clay.) Let the
clay dry. Paint your creatures strong
colors. Paint on eyes, spots
or stripes.

Lucky cat money box

1 The clay mold

Shape a waving cat from clay. Keep it simple. Let the cat dry. Cover it with plastic wrap and rub on a layer of petroleum jelly.

2 The papier mâché mold

Cover the cat with five layers of papier mâché. (See page 7.) Let it dry overnight.

3 Cutting the mold

Ask an adult to cut the dry papier mâché mould in half. Remove the clay cat. Join the halves with papier mâché strips.

4 The base

Draw around the base of the cat on cardboard. Cut it out and tape it onto the cat. Paste a layer of papier mâché over the joins. Ask an adult to help you cut a slit in the cat's head.

5 Painting

Paint the cat white. Add eyes, a nose, paws and colorful decorations.

Spotty animals

Shape a piece of self-hardening clay into the body of an animal. Add a head, legs and a tail. (See page 6 for instructions for joining two pieces of clay.) Let the animal dry completely and paint it white.

When the paint is dry, add colorful spots, the eyes and a nose.

Wheels and waves

Some toy cars, boats and trucks are exact
copies of the real thing. They are
interesting to look at and fun to play with.
You can imagine you are traveling to
faraway places.

In ancient Egypt, people believed
that, when they died, their spirit
traveled to another land. In their
tombs, Egyptians buried models of
things they would need in the next
world. These included small boats
with model sailors hard at work.

In the picture above, the owner of
the boat is sitting under a canopy.
The sailor at the front is checking to see
how deep the water is. The men with
poles are pushing the boat off a
sandbank. The person at the back is
steering with a long oar.

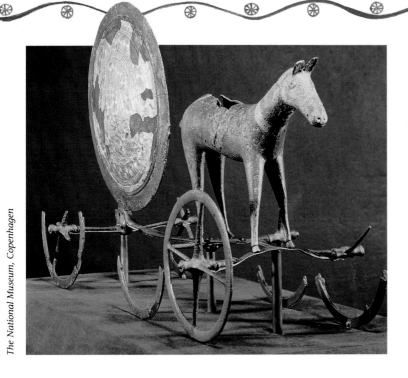

The National Museum, Copenhagen

This bronze model of the sun riding in a horse-drawn chariot is over three thousand years old. It was found in a swamp in Denmark about a hundred years ago. No one knows exactly why it was made. Some people think it was used in religious ceremonies.

In Kenya, children make toy bicycles from recycled wire. The riders are made of stuffed cloth.

In Ecuador and Colombia, people make clay models of open-sided buses. They are filled with people going to market, carrying baskets of fruit and vegetables.

Many people on the small islands of Indonesia make their living from fishing. Young boys build models of fishing boats as toys.

By the time the boys are old enough to go fishing themselves, they know how to build and sail full-size boats.

James Davis Travel Photography

Recycled racers

Think how you would like to travel. You might skim over the water in a sail boat, drive a slow tractor or race a golden chariot. Recycle bits and pieces you find at home to make models of some of your favorite ways of traveling.

Bottle boat

Lay two empty plastic pop bottles, with their caps on, side by side. Leave a small space between them. Ask an adult to cut a piece of thick cardboard or balsa wood, big enough to fit as a deck on top of the bottles.

Ask an adult to cut a small hole in the center of the deck, close to the top ends of the bottles. Stick the deck to the bottles with waterproof glue.

Glue two smaller sticks to a tall mast, as shown in the picture. Tie string where the sticks and the mast join to hold them together.

Cut a cloth sail and glue it over the sticks. Push the mast into the hole in the deck. Attach the mast to the deck with masking tape.

Cardboard tractor

Collect small cardboard boxes. Glue or tape them together to make a tractor. You can cut out windows and doors. Collect two barbecue sticks or two bamboo garden sticks. They will be the axles. Use the tops of four plastic containers as wheels. Make holes in the plastic tops large enough for the axles to go through. Don't attach the wheels and axles yet.

Cut a piece of thin cardboard ¾ inches (2 cm) by 2 inches (5 cm). Draw two lines with a ballpoint pen and ruler, as shown. Press hard to dent the cardboard.

Bend the cardboard into a bridge, like this. Make three more bridges. Lay the axles in position on the bottom of the tractor. Place the bridges over the axles and glue or tape them down. Push the wheels onto the axles.

wheel
'bridge'
axle

Sun chariot

Cut out a square of thick cardboard. (You may need an adult to help you.) Tape on sides and a front. (See page 7 for instructions for joining cardboard.) Cut out a sun, birds or animals from another piece of cardboard. Glue them onto the chariot. Paint everything sunny colors. Cut out four wheels. Cut out or paint on spokes. Attach the wheels to the chariot in the same way the wheels are attached to the tractor. (See above.)

Imaginary creatures

Throughout history, people have imagined all sorts of amazing creatures. Some are part-animal and part-human. Others are a mixture of two or more animals. Some have two or even three heads.

There are many myths about mermaids—creatures that are half-woman, half-fish. They have flowing hair and scaly fish tails. They live in a palace at the bottom of the sea.

Mermaids are very beautiful. In some stories, they hold a mirror in one hand and a comb in the other. They have wonderful voices and lure sailors onto rocks with their singing.

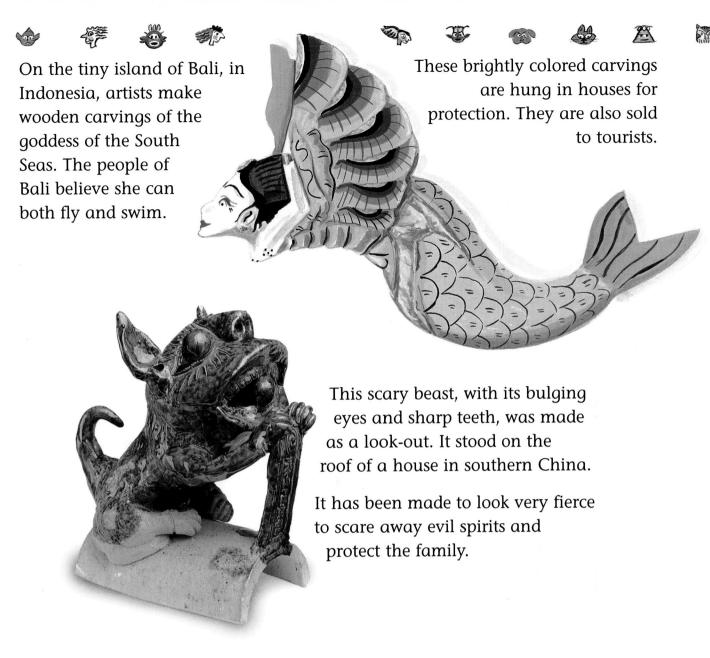

On the tiny island of Bali, in Indonesia, artists make wooden carvings of the goddess of the South Seas. The people of Bali believe she can both fly and swim.

These brightly colored carvings are hung in houses for protection. They are also sold to tourists.

This scary beast, with its bulging eyes and sharp teeth, was made as a look-out. It stood on the roof of a house in southern China.

It has been made to look very fierce to scare away evil spirits and protect the family.

The Kongo people of Central Africa carved special figures, like this two-headed dog, which they called *nkonde*. The spirit of the *nkonde*, which means hunter, was believed to track down evil people.

When people had a problem, they would tell the *nkonde* and hammer a nail or a sharp piece of metal into its body. This was supposed to anger the *nkonde* into using its special powers.

Photo: P. A. Ferrazini. Musée Barbier-Mueller, Geneva

Fierce and fantastic

Close your eyes and imagine a fierce monster, a two-headed dog or a creature that is half-animal and half-human. Imagine a mermaid with a scaly fish tail. Now open your eyes and create these strange creatures yourself.

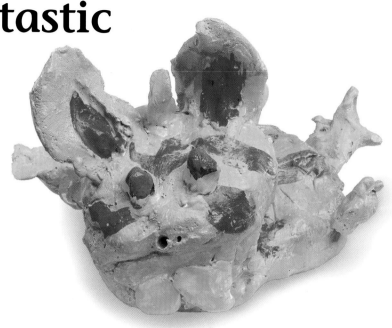

Great guard monsters

Shape the head and body of a monster from self-hardening clay. Add legs and a tail. (See page 6 for instructions for joining two pieces of clay.) Give your monster horns, spikes, sharp teeth and a long tongue.

Let the clay dry. Paint your monster.

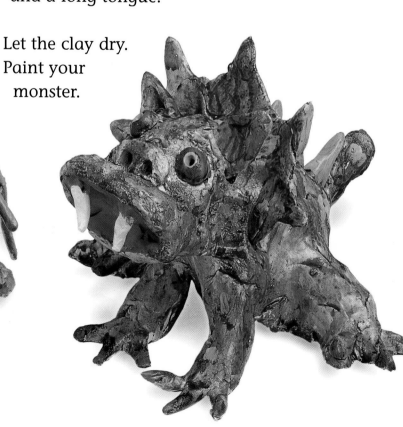

Two-headed terrors

Shape colored salt dough into a creature with two heads. (See page 6 for instructions for how to make salt dough.) Make it look really wild. Push nails, paper clips, sticks, dry beans and pasta into the dough.

Bake your creature on a greased baking sheet. (See page 6 for instructions.) Ask an adult to help you. Let your monster cool before you touch it.

Strange sea creatures

Shape a mermaid from self-hardening clay. Make little clay decorations and attach them to your mermaid with toothpicks. When the clay is dry, paint your mermaid wild colors. Make other sea creatures in the same way.

Models in action

Some models move. They slide on and off a toy stage. Others have moving parts. Some have heads that wag and arms that wave.

One hundred and fifty years ago, families had fun playing with model theaters. The small, wooden stage was a copy of a real theater. The scenery and costumes were all copied from real plays.

The scenery and characters were printed onto sheets of paper. The main characters came in different costumes so they could be used in different scenes in the play. Children cut them out and glued them onto cardboard.

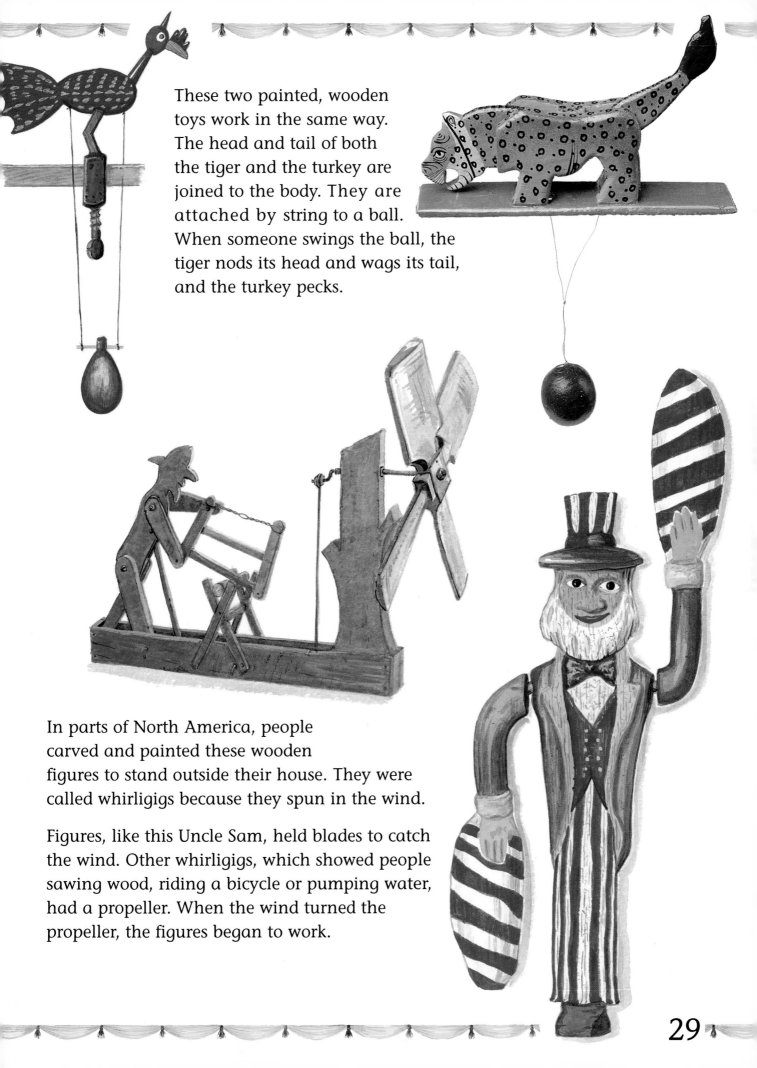

These two painted, wooden toys work in the same way. The head and tail of both the tiger and the turkey are joined to the body. They are attached by string to a ball. When someone swings the ball, the tiger nods its head and wags its tail, and the turkey pecks.

In parts of North America, people carved and painted these wooden figures to stand outside their house. They were called whirligigs because they spun in the wind.

Figures, like this Uncle Sam, held blades to catch the wind. Other whirligigs, which showed people sawing wood, riding a bicycle or pumping water, had a propeller. When the wind turned the propeller, the figures began to work.

Moving models

You, too, can design a toy theater and perform your own plays. You can also make a model of a dog with a moving head and tail.

Toy theater

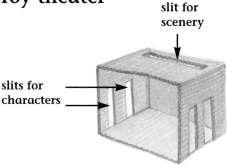

slit for scenery

slits for characters

1 The stage

Cut off the flaps of a cardboard box and turn it on its side. Ask an adult to help you cut slits in it, as shown above.

This hole should be slightly smaller than the stage front

2 The arch

On stiff cardboard, draw a fancy arch and a platform to fit the front of the box. Make sure the opening of the arch is smaller than the front of the box. Cut out the arch and the platform. Stick them onto the box with masking tape. (See page 7.) Paint the theater bright colors.

3 Scenery

Cut out several pieces of cardboard 1 inch (2 cm) taller and ½ inch (1 cm) narrower than the box. Paint on different scenes.

4 Characters

Draw characters and long stick-shapes on cardboard. Cut them out and color them. Tape the back of each character to the end of a cardboard stick.

Nodding doggy

Ask an adult to help with this project.

1 Roll a small ball of self-hardening clay. Make a hole through the middle. Paint the ball when the clay is dry.

2 On thick cardboard, draw a head, four bodies, a tail and a base. Cut them out. Glue two body pieces together. Do the same to the other two.

3 Make holes in the head, bodies and tail. Those in the bodies must be small enough for a wooden barbecue stick to fit tightly. Those in the head and tail must be large enough for the stick to fit loosely. Paint your dog white.

4 Cut four pieces of thick cardboard, ½ inch (1 cm) by ¾ inch (2 cm). Glue them together to make a wedge.

5 Glue the wedge between the bodies. Glue and tape the legs onto the base.

6 Paint spots and a face on the dog.

7 Push a dressmaker's pin into the back of the head and the tail, as shown.

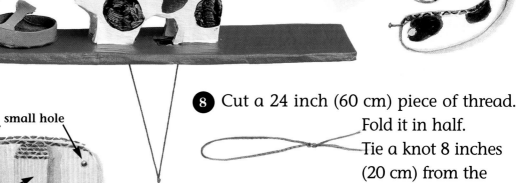

8 Cut a 24 inch (60 cm) piece of thread. Fold it in half. Tie a knot 8 inches (20 cm) from the ends. Thread the looped end through the hole in the ball. Push the open ends through the loop.

9 Push one of the ends of the thread through the front hole in the bottom of the base. Pull the thread through and tie it to the pin on the head. Push the other end through the back hole in the base and tie it to the tail pin.

10 Hold the head between the two body pieces. Push a wooden barbecue stick through the holes. Trim the ends of the stick. Do the same with the tail.

Swing the ball around to move your dog!

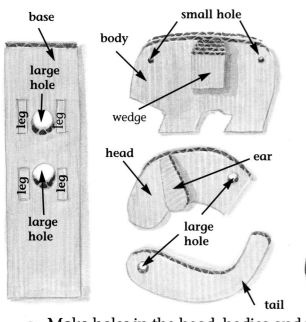

base

large hole

leg   leg

leg   leg

large hole

body

small hole

wedge

head

ear

large hole

tail

Index

Africa, **25**

animal, **4, 16, 17, 18, 19, 23, 24, 26**

army, **8**

axle, **23**

Bali, **25**

battlefield, **8**

bicycle, **21, 29**

boat, **4, 20, 21, 22**

building, **4, 12, 13**

bus, **21**

car, **4, 20, 23**

chair, **4, 14**

chariot, **21, 22, 23**

chess pieces, **8**

China, **13, 25**

clay, **5, 6, 11, 14, 17, 18, 21, 26, 27, 31**

Colombia, **21**

decoy, **17**

Denmark, **21**

dog, **30, 31**

doll, **8, 9, 10, 13**

dolls' house, **4, 12**

Ecuador, **21**

Egypt, **20**

fishing, **21**

furniture, **4, 12, 14**

Germany, **9**

hemming, **7, 10**

Hopi, **9**

horse, **8, 17, 21**

Indonesia, **21, 25**

Japan, **17**

kachina doll, **9, 10, 11**

Kenya, **21**

kitchen, **12**

Kongo, **25**

lucky cat, **17, 18, 19**

mermaid, **24, 26, 27**

Mexico, **16**

model theater, **28, 30**

monster, **26, 27**

Native North Americans, **13, 17**

nkonde, **25**

North America, **29**

papier mâché, **7, 17, 19**

peddler doll, **9, 10**

Peru, **9**

retablo, **9**

running stitch, **7, 10**

Russia, **17**

sailor, **4, 20, 24**

saint, **9**

salt dough, **5, 6, 11, 27**

spirit, **4, 9, 13, 20, 25**

spirit house, **13, 14, 15**

story box, **10, 11**

sun god, **17**

table, **4, 14**

temple, **13**

Thailand, **13**

tepee, **13, 14, 15**

tomb, **12, 13, 20**

toy, **4, 12, 16, 17, 21, 28, 29**

tractor, **22, 23**

Uncle Sam, **29**

whirligig, **29**

wood, **5, 16, 18, 22, 29**

wood carving, **16, 25**

Acknowledgements

The authors and publishers are grateful to the following people for their help with this book:
Kristin Baybars, 7 Mansfield Road, London NW3 2JD Tel: 0171 267 0934 supplier of dolls' house furniture; Paul Williams, Department of Theology and Religious Studies, Bristol University; Alison Seman, Jonathan Brown, Abeno, Okonomi-Yaki restaurant, Yoahan Plaza, London.